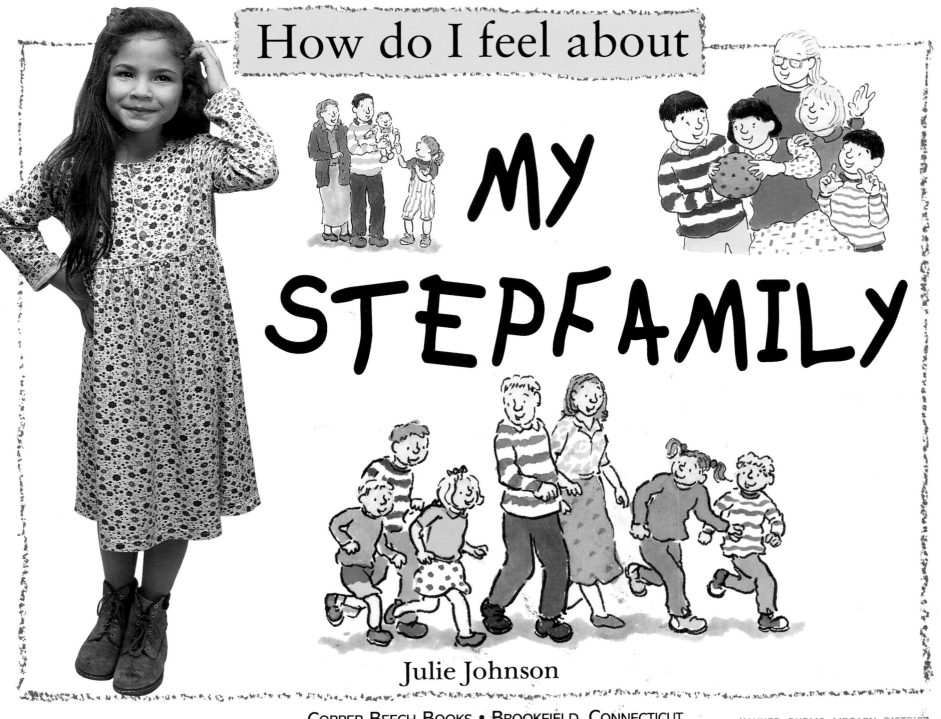

How do I feel about

MY STEPFAMILY

Julie Johnson

COPPER BEECH BOOKS • BROOKFIELD, CONNECTICUT

Designed and produced by
Aladdin Books Ltd
28 Percy Street
London W1P 0LD

First published in the United States
in 1998 by
Copper Beech Books,
an imprint of
The Millbrook Press
2 Old New Milford Road
Brookfield, Connecticut 06804

Printed in Belgium
5 4 3 2 1

Designer   Tessa Barwick
Editor   Sarah Levete
Illustrator   Christopher
                    O'Neill
Photographer   Roger Vlitos

**Library of Congress
Cataloging-in-Publication Data**
Johnson, Julie.
How do I feel about my stepfamily /
Julie Johnson ; illustrated by Christopher O'Neill.
p. cm. — (How do I feel about)
Includes index.
Summary: Young people in stepfamilies describe
how they cope with having stepbrothers, stepsisters,
and stepparents and offer tips on dealing with
change in your family.
ISBN 0-7613-0868-7 (lib. bdg.)
1. Stepfamilies—Juvenile literature.
[1. Stepfamilies.] I. O'Neill, Christopher.
II. Title. III. Series
HQ759.92.J65 1998   98-16957
306.874—dc21   CIP AC

Contents

Introduction

Molly, Tom, Ali, and Gary are friends. Each one of them is a member of a stepfamily. Families come in many different shapes and sizes. Stepfamilies are just one kind of family. The four friends will share their thoughts and feelings about having a stepparent, stepbrothers, and stepsisters.

What are Stepfamilies?

Ali's dad and mom split up a few years ago. Ali's dad has a new partner named Kate. Kate is Ali's stepmom. Molly is telling Ali that being a member of a stepfamily is just like being in any family except that a stepfamily is made from two families, or one family and another grown-up.

> In my stepfamily, there's me, my stepmom, and my dad.

> Jo is going to be your stepmom.

> My stepfamily's almost big enough to be a soccer team!

You may have a stepparent… 4 *…and stepbrothers and sisters.*

▼ Two Moms?

A stepfamily is the coming together of two adults, one or both of whom have children from a previous relationship. This means that you may have two moms — your natural mom and a stepmom. You can love them both in different ways.

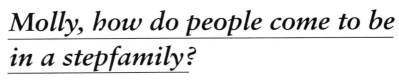

It's great isn't it?

Yeah. I've never done this before.

◄ Little Or Large?

A stepfamily may be small or quite large if your stepparent already has his or her own children. If both your parents have new partners, you may even have two stepfamilies!

Molly, *how do people come to be in a stepfamily?*

"Stepfamilies can happen for lots of reasons. Dad died when I was a baby. Then Mom married Paul, my stepdad. My sister, Mom, and I went to live with Paul and his children. Ali has a stepfamily because her parents split up and her dad remarried."

Stepparents

Tom is telling Ali how much he enjoys his regular visits to see his mom, stepdad, and stepbrothers. For most of the time, Tom lives with his natural dad and he gets along really well with his stepdad, too. But you may be more like Ali. It took her a long time to accept and to like her stepmom.

At first, I was angry with my stepmom for not being my natural mom. But now I know I can love them both.

No, I don't need any help.

I got along well with my stepdad right away. He's really nice.

Accepting new people can be hard...

6

...or it can be easy and fun!

▽ *I Miss My Mom*

You may blame your stepparent for your natural parents splitting up. It's quite natural to feel like this. But try to remember that blaming people or feeling angry won't change the situation.

◁ *Help!*

For some grown-ups, becoming a stepparent is their first attempt at being a parent. Your stepparent may be worried about how you will all get along and if you like them. Try to remember that grown-ups can feel nervous, too!

▷ *I'm Confused!*

You may feel confused if you love your natural parent, but also get along well with your new stepparent. Your natural mom or dad will always be special to you, but it is not wrong to care about your new parent. You can love people in different ways.

1. Mark thinks that his mom will stop loving Colin, his stepdad, if he is unfriendly to him.

2. Mark tells his mom that he doesn't like Colin because he's not his natural dad.

3. Colin tries to make friends with Mark but nothing seems to work.

Why is Mark being so unfriendly?

Mark misses his natural dad and is determined not to like Colin. He feels that Colin is trying to take the place of his dad. But being unfriendly to Colin will not make his mom and his natural dad get back together. Colin doesn't want to take the place of Mark's dad. He just wants to be a good friend to Mark.

▼ Two Sets Of Parents!

If you live with your stepfamily you may also want to spend time with the parent from whom you live apart. This is not always possible, but remember that it's OK to love your stepparent and your natural parent.

I'll never like Paul because he's not my real dad.

◄ Feelings

If you find it very hard to accept or to like your stepparent, tell your other parent how you feel. Talking about your feelings doesn't make a problem go away, but it can help to make you feel better.

I do get along with my stepmom but it's so nice when I spend time with my mom.

Ali, *how do you feel about having a mom and a stepmom?*

"At first I didn't want to like Kate, my stepmom, because I missed my natural mom. But Mom explained that I can love them in different ways. I still see my mom on weekends and she'll always be my mom. We have a great time together but I can have a good time with Kate, too."

Stepbrothers and Sisters

Molly and Tom both have stepbrothers and sisters, as well as their own natural brothers and sisters. It can take time to get used to having a stepbrother or sister. Remember that stepbrothers and sisters can fall out and be best of friends, just like any brothers and sisters!

It's not always easy to join in.

You may feel angry at all the changes.

▽ *Quiet Time*

You may sometimes want to spend some quiet time with your natural mom or dad, rather than always seeing him or her with your stepbrothers or sisters. There is nothing wrong in wanting to do this.

Nobody listens to me anymore.

◁ *What About Me?*

Having new stepbrothers and sisters can mean that you suddenly have to share your natural parent with lots of other people. This may make you feel angry and a bit jealous, too.

▷ *Feeling Left Out*

If you feel left out or find it hard to get along with your stepbrothers or sisters, tell your natural parent or stepparent how you feel. They may not be able to make the problem go away immediately, but it can help to tell someone how you feel.

I can understand you feeling left out. I'm glad you told me.

1. Before Dan and his daughter, Rosie, moved in, Polly had her own room.

2. Polly felt really angry when Rosie moved into her room.

3. After a while, they got used to sharing a room. They even enjoyed it!

Why didn't Polly want to share her room with Rosie?

Polly didn't ask for a stepsister, but she got one, and she had to share her room with her! Sharing things with a stepbrother or sister can be hard if, like Polly, you have not had to do so before. It's not easy accepting situations that you have not chosen, but sometimes they work out better than you think!

▽ *Why Can't I Choose?*

Some stepbrothers and sisters hit it off right away. It may be that you have not liked being an only child and now have someone to spend time with. A stepbrother or sister can become a good friend.

We don't want you to play with us.

◁ *Help Make It Easy*

If you are a member of a large family and a stepbrother or sister comes to visit or to stay with you, make an effort to include him or her in your games. You may not be best friends, but it helps to be friendly.

It's great having a sister to do things with now.

Molly, how do you get along with your stepbrothers and stepsisters.

"At first my sister and I didn't like them. But we all tried really hard and we get along most of the time now. It's nice having Emma, who is older than I am. It's fun playing football with the boys but they can be a pain at times, just like all brothers."

13

Getting Used to Change

When Gary and his dad moved in with Gary's stepmom, Gary had to go to a new school. He had to get used to a different way of doing things with his dad and stepmom, and another way of doing things with his mom and stepdad! Becoming part of a stepfamily can mean lots of changes.

You may have to move.

Things may be different.

▼ *A New School!*

A new family may also mean moving and going to a new school. Going to a new school can be difficult, especially if you join in the middle of a school year. All changes take a while to get used to.

Lauren is coming to live with us.

◄ *It's Our House!*

Sharing your home with a stepfamily can mean lots of changes. You may not like all of them. You may feel angry if no one asked you how you would feel about it. Try to remember that it's also strange for your new stepfamily.

► *What Do I Call Her?*

It can be difficult knowing what to call your stepparent. He or she is not your natural parent, and you may not want to call him or her Dad or Mom. It is a good idea to talk about it together so that you can decide what feels right for all of you.

What am I going to call my new mom?

1. Keith's dad has come to pick Keith up for their weekly day out together.

2. Keith enjoys being with his dad, who lives with Jan, his new partner.

3. Keith was upset when his dad said that he could not see him next Saturday.

Why was Keith disappointed?

Keith lives with his mom and sees his dad once a week. He enjoys being with his dad. The time you spend with the parent from whom you live apart is important. It can make you feel let down, upset, and angry if he or she is unable to see you. This feeling is quite natural.

▼ New Babies!

A new baby can mean lots of change, even if the baby is your natural brother or sister. But a new baby doesn't mean that your natural parent and your stepparent are going to stop loving you.

I think you've had enough candy for one day!

But my mom never takes my candy away.

Susan is going to have a baby.

◄ It's All Different Now!

You may find it difficult if your stepparent does not let you behave in the same way as your natural parent does. Try to tell both parents how you feel so you can all agree on what you are, or are not, allowed to do.

Gary, how did you cope with all the changes?

"To begin with, it was so confusing and I felt angry that everything had to change. Nothing was the same. But it was lots of change for everyone. Even though it was all scary, it was quite fun too."

Being a Family

Last week in class Tom and Molly were talking about what it means to be part of a family. They decided that in some ways being part of a stepfamily is not really that different from being part of any other family, except that you come together from two families.

There can be bad days...

18

...and there can be good days!

◁ Sharing

I want to play with that.

I had it first!

In all families everybody has to learn to get along. Some people find it easier than others. In a stepfamily, just like in any other family, there will be times when you get fed up with each other.

My dad lets me watch T.V. whenever I want.

But Mom, you only let me watch an hour of T.V. a day.

▷ Speak Up

Talking and listening to each other is important for all families. It can be especially important as members of a stepfamily get used to each other. Sorting out any difficulties is much easier if you talk to each other.

△ Feeling Jealous

It is quite natural for you to feel a little jealous of a stepbrother or sister. It may seem as if he or she is given special treatment by your parents. Try to remember that it takes time for everyone to get used to being in a stepfamily.

Being a Family

1. The Brooks family were trying to organize a day out.

2. Anne decided to write down what each person wanted to do.

3. Anne's plan meant that everyone would be happy.

How did Anne manage to please everyone?

Anne's stepfamily all wanted to do something different. She decided to make a list of what each person wanted to do. That way, they worked out a plan that made everyone happy. Being part of a family is much easier and more fun if you all take time to think of each other.

▽ *Good Times!*

It can be a lot of fun doing things together as a family and that means a stepfamily, too! You can still enjoy being part of a stepfamily, even if you only see your stepfamily from time to time.

It's your fault!

No, it's not. You did it!

Wah, wah!

◁ *Not So Good Times!*

All families have times when they get fed up with each other. But you'll feel much better about it if you don't stay angry for too long. Remember the good times and try to learn from the difficult times.

Tom, do you find it hard seeing your stepfamily only on weekends?

"It's not a problem. I love living with Dad but it's a lot of fun going to stay with my stepfamily, as well. It can take a while before I feel really at home when I go to visit my stepfamily, but after that it's just like being in any family."

Don't Forget . . .

Ali, *what tips do you have about new stepparents?*

"I was really upset about my parents splitting up. I didn't want to speak to Kate, my stepmom. But when I realized that my mom and dad were not going to get back together, I started to give Kate a chance. She's like a friend now."

Tom, *what tips do you have for getting along with stepbrothers and sisters?*

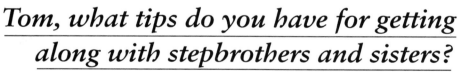

"Give them a chance because they probably feel as unsure about you as you do about them. Try not to decide right away whether you like them or not. You may never be best of friends with them, but then again you may. You may even get along with them better than your natural brothers or sisters. And if you have any problems, talk about them."

Gary, what do you think about all the changes you have had to make?

"I was quite angry when Dad first told me that I had to move, change school, and have a stepmom. But we had a talk and he said he was as nervous as I was about all the changes. It made it better because we both felt the same."

I'll be sharing my dad now, but I'll have a new mom as well.

I'll miss my old house.

But I'll write to my old friends.

I'm sure I'll like my new school.

Molly, have you got any tips for new stepfamilies?

"Try to accept the situation. It may be much better than you think. In any family, you need to work together and to talk about any problems. If you do feel uncomfortable, tell your natural parent or another grown-up who you trust."

Index

All the photographs in this book have been posed by models. The publishers would like to thank them all.